Are You Sure You Can Manage?

Software Engineering Management
from the Software Engineers' Perspective.

by Marcus Tomlinson

DEDICATION

To my son Aaron, without whom this book would not have been so short :)

CONTENTS

Part One: Manage Your...

Part Three: Manage Their...

ABOUT THE AUTHOR

Marcus Tomlinson is a qualified BSc Software Engineer from Durban, South Africa, with well over a decade of experience in embedded and non-embedded software development.

Immediately following his university career, Marcus landed his first job at Africa's leading manufacturer of electronic security products: IDS, where at the age of 21, he co-created a revolutionary new, modular test jig system to help the company keep up with its rapidly growing product demand (A system that is still in effect today).

At 25, he went on to land his first senior development role at the world's largest supplier of military and mining simulators: ThoroughTec, making him the youngest employee to hold the position. During his time there,

Marcus completely and independently overhauled the company's internal audio engine, as well as created a highly successful data-flow framework called CircuitSim, to modularise and simulate complex vehicle control systems.

In late 2013, Marcus landed a job at the open source software giant: Canonical, designing and developing Ubuntu's Unity Shell. From 2013 to 2016, he steadily rose up the ranks from Engineer to Technical Lead on the Ubuntu Personal team, and has presented at a number of Open Source Developer Summits.

PREFACE

As an engineer, ever found yourself asking the question: "What the heck is my manager doing?!". I have, many times. Perhaps you're on your way to becoming a manager yourself, in which case you might be asking: "What the heck am I getting myself into?!". Of course, if you're a manager already, chances are you've asked yourself at least once: "What the heck am I doing wrong?!". No matter how you put it, the question on all of our minds at some point has been: "What *should* the manager be doing?".

Throughout my career, I've always been fascinated with the complex sociology behind successful (and unsuccessful) engineering teams. I've read many books on the topic, and spent loads of time picking the brains of my teammates and managers, but I anticipated that, unless I spent some time trying to understand what it's like to be the manager myself, few would take what I had to say seriously. So, while my interest in engineering processes and team dynamics has earned me a number of unofficial leadership positions over the last 10 years, I figured it was time I took on a full-time role.

2 years ago I started small by asking if I could run the team's morning meeting. Over the next few months, as I continued to prove myself, my responsibilities extended to delegating and following up on tasks, representing the team in various stakeholder meetings, and leading the development of a major project from start to finish. It wasn't long before I was promoted to Tech Lead, where I experienced many more management-level ups and downs, from turning failing projects and their teams around, to assisting in some tough decisions to let people go.

As Tech Lead, I found myself in the unique situation of being almost as much a part of management as I was a part of engineering. I couldn't imagine a better position to finally be answering the question: "What *should* the manager be doing?". It may seem obvious that in order to judge the manager, one should have at least some understanding of what it's like to be him, but in the end, it's not the manager who decides whether he's effective or not. While engineers may not choose who their managers are, they sure as heck will choose who their leaders are.

Which brings us to the topic of this book. The only good way to answer the elusive: "What *should* the manager be doing?", is to first answer the question: "What do great engineers expect from their managers?", then leave it to you to determine how much of it you do (or your manager does) effectively.

Let's begin by taking a look at what I, as an engineer, expect my manager's job to entail at a minimum:

Manage Yourself
Understand what it takes to be a manager, know how to manage yourself, lead by example, and keep composure when things get tough.

Manage Your Boss
Understand your boss's expectations, keep him happy, and let him know when things go wrong.

Manage Your Peers

Study the company org chart, make the right connections, and maintain those connections.

Manage The Outsiders

Be on the lookout for great engineers, know how to read their résumés, interview the promising ones, hire the right ones, and get them integrated into the team.

Manage The Engineers

Get to know your engineers, hold weekly one-on-ones with them, conduct their annual performance reviews, motivate them, handle their emotional outbursts, deal with those who want to leave, and deal with those who should leave.

Manage The Team

Develop a culture of excellence in the team, get them pulling in the same direction, keep communication flowing, protect them from others, and protect them from themselves.

Manage Their Environment

Recognise an unhealthy work environment, and create an environment that works.

Manage Their Projects

Align yourself with the company's strategy, get projects off on the right foot, keep development rolling, monitor progress, and handle disasters.

Consequently, this is how I've chosen to structure the book. Armed with a rough idea of what the manager is responsible for, let's dig a little deeper into what I (and the many engineers I've worked with) believe each of these responsibilities *should* involve...

PART ONE

Manage Your...

CHAPTER ONE
Yourself

1.1. Understand what it takes to be a manager

- Development to management is not a promotion, it's a career restart. Very few skills are transferable.

- Situational adaptability is essential. What worked in one context may not work in another.

- You'll need a skill in packaging complex ideas into easy-to-consume reports and presentations.

- Communication is a massive part of the job, so you'll need to be an exceptional communicator.

- If the engineers knew your motivation behind becoming a manager, would they still respect you?

1.2. Know how to manage yourself

- Your boss will be more concerned with managing upward, so you'll need to manage yourself.

- For meetings, arrive on time, and leave on time. For workdays, arrive first, and leave last.

- Keep a running to-do list. Taking notes and turning them into tasks is a key part of your job.

- Every morning, set out your objectives for the day, and prioritise what is both urgent and important.

- Don't overcommit. Block off at least an hour a week for yourself, and skip unnecessary meetings.

- You are one, they are many, so listen more and talk less.

1.3. Lead by example

- By example is the only way you can influence others, and it happens whether you like it or not.

- You'll need to earn and maintain the technical respect of those you manage.

- Lead by ethical example: Be approachable, empathetic, fair, honest, humble, and positive.

- You'll need to be genuinely passionate about the work your team does.

- Great leaders are authentic, not "perfect". Smart people won't allow themselves to be led by a fake.

1.4. Keep composure when things get tough

- It can get lonely being a manager. You're no longer a peer to your engineers, you're their boss.

- Getting too chummy with some can alienate others. Start distant and grow closer with caution.

- A good manager not only understands his weaknesses, he entrusts his staff to fill them.

- When something irritates you, avoid emotional outbursts, let it soak and come back to it later.

- If you're unsure whether or not you're doing a good job, ask yourself, do people trust me?

Summary

- Understand what it takes to be a manager.
- Know how to manage yourself.
- Lead by example.
- Keep composure when things get tough.

CHAPTER TWO
Your Boss

2.1. Understand your boss's expectations

- Not only should you manage your team well, you need to convince your boss that you're doing it.

- Understand the kind of person your boss is, and the background he's from. Speak his language.

- You have another boss: The client. Remember, clients have the power to fire everyone.

2.2. Keep him happy

- Not only is keeping the boss happy beneficial to

you, you represent the team, so they benefit too.

- Find ways to make your boss's job easier, but don't step on his toes to do it.

- Report only as regularly as your boss expects you to. When you do, be clear, concise, and honest.

- Under-promise and over-deliver to your boss (clients included).

2.3. Let him know when things go wrong

- When problems are starting to arise that the boss should know about, report them immediately.

- It's your job to raise concern about bad ideas. Even when your boss is the one suggesting them.

Summary

- Understand your boss's expectations.
- Keep him happy.
- Let him know when things go wrong.

Are You Sure You Can Manage?

CHAPTER THREE
Your Peers

3.1. Study the company org chart

- Part of your job is to communicate and facilitate communication in all directions of the org chart.

- Forming a close network of peers can make your job easier, and your boss's job easier too.

- Well-connected managers are well-informed. They're quick to react when things change.

- A company's combined experience can only really be capitalised on by the management "team".

3.2. Make the right connections

- The heads of other teams and departments can help you connect the right people together.

- Internal recruiters may go beyond in trying to understand complex requirements for a new hire.

- Other managers you respect can make great role models to learn from.

- HR can help with justly compensating your top performers, and with handling the difficult ones.

- Finance can help you more effectively manage within budget. They may even help you stretch it.

- Legal can be a massive help in understanding complex contracts, licences, and patents.

3.3. Maintain those connections

- Find ways to make their job easier. They'll be more inclined to return the favour at a later stage.

- You need to gain acceptance by conforming to a company's norms before you can challenge them.

- Find opportunities to converse formally and informally. When you do, speak their language.

- Be sincere in your attempt to befriend them, and look out for signs that the connection is fading.

Summary

- Study the company org chart.
- Make the right connections.
- Maintain those connections.

PART TWO

Manage The...

CHAPTER FOUR
The Outsiders

4.1. Be on the lookout for great engineers

- Keep a contact list of every promising engineer you meet. Whether you're hiring or not.

- Before seeking out a new hire, prepare to prove that you've considered other alternatives.

- You can only use as many engineers as there are parallel pieces of work to be done.

- When compiling the job listing, be as specific as possible about what it is you're looking for.

- First consider internal referrals, then try low-cost advertising, then resort to external recruiters.

4.2. Know how to read their résumés

- A résumé should at least match the job requirements, but check against LinkedIn as well.

- Don't take education too seriously, experience (especially personal projects) is more important.

- A well-written résumé can be a good indication of one's ability to write good documentation.

- Take note of any possible red flags or ambiguities you'd like to clear up during the interviews.

4.3. Interview the promising ones

- Try to evaluate logical and technical ability, social skills, enthusiasm to grow, and team approval.

- Assemble a small team of interviewers, and work together on a series of questions and exercises.

- Candidates will blur together. Judge them against the same criteria and keep notes to compare.

- During the first call, ask questions about their previous job, and their expectations of their next.

- Keep interviews conversational, prefer open-ended questions, and avoid gotchas or IQ tests.

- A coding exercise can be useful. Have it include design, set a deadline, but don't surveil them.

- To evaluate team approval, have the candidate present some previous related work to the team.

- Take note of those who ask great questions, teach you something, and somehow just feel right.

4.4. Hire the right ones

- Hiring the right engineer is hard to do, but hiring the wrong one is even harder to undo.

- Before making an offer, check the candidate's

references, but not just the ones they gave you.

- Avoid creating inequities in the team by offering too high (or low). Know when to cut your losses.

- Candidates hesitant to accept don't necessarily want more pay, they may want an elevated role.

- Keep in contact between the offer and their first day. Send them info, but don't overwhelm them.

4.5. Get them integrated into the team

- Short-term contractors are not part of the team. Keep a rein on them. Don't allow ramp-up time.

- For the first few days, make the hire feel welcome, and a part of a great team with great projects.

- On the morning of their first day, have a buddy introduce them to various VIPs (incl. HR & IT).

- In the afternoon, get them right onto achievable tasks such as building and testing the project.

- By the end of his probation, was he competent, accepted, timely, vocal, inquisitive, and humble?

Summary

- Be on the lookout for great engineers.
- Know how to read their résumés.
- Interview the promising ones.
- Hire the right ones.
- Get them integrated into the team.

CHAPTER FIVE

The Engineers

5.1. Get to know your engineers

• Some developers can clearly see the forest, some can clearly see the trees, but few can see both.

• Programmers usually stick to one type of development: client, server, DB, or web/scripting.

• There are 3 main types of developer: application programmer, system programmer, and architect.

• A mix of programmers from various domains means unique ways of seeing the same problem.

- Some other personality types include: left/right-brained, cowboys, heroes, introverts, and jerks.

- While there are ways to categorise a programmer, every person is unique and unpredictable.

5.2. Hold weekly one-on-ones with them

- Schedule a 30min one-on-one with each engineer every week on the same day, and try not to cancel.

- Aim to learn something, don't cover data that can be found elsewhere, and no written reports!

- Strike a balance between formal and informal dialogue. Ease in with a simple: "How are you?".

- Allow the smallest voice to be heard, measure real progress, and give feedback on performance.

- Show an interest in your staff, and keep notes as not to forget details from previous conversations.

5.3. Conduct their annual performance reviews

- During performance reviews is possibly the worse time of the year for you yourself to be tardy.

- The typical schedule: self review, peer reviews (optional), your review, meet, sign, submit to HR.

- Try to deliver feedback in a positive way. Keep negativity to a minimum, but prefer to avoid it.

- An average engineer does what's asked, a good one does it well, and a great one surprises you.

- Promote people who have already proven they deserve it, and don't only promote those who ask.

5.4. Motivate them

- Programmers enjoy programming. When they don't, it may be an error in your management.

- A developer's needs must be satisfied before he can be motivated.

- Needs include: Respect for the manager, career development, a good environment, and money.

- Not satisfying a need is a demotivator, but needs are not motivators themselves.

- Motivators include: Autonomy, mastery, purpose, and (a big one) recognition.

- Motivators do not include: The shareholders' interests, scheduled rewarding, and pressure.

5.5. Handle their emotional outbursts

- The only suitable way to address a controversy is face-to-face. Not via email or IM.

- Don't participate in the outburst. The worst reaction you can have is any sort of emotion.

- Give the person the benefit of the doubt, be empathetic, ask questions, and do lots of listening.

- If the outburst is irrational, the best you can do is

ease them into wanting to solve it themselves.

- Managers develop their social skills on the job but forget that it's rarely an engineer's strength.

5.6. Deal with those who want to leave

- Some people leave to start businesses. See if you can offer what they're chasing, in their job.

- Ask your staff if they're bored. People can only be bored for so long before they'll want to leave.

- Ask your staff if they're tired. People can only go full steam for so long before they'll burn out.

- People leave when they feel undervalued. Treat them as investments by actually investing in them.

- When good engineers leave, the people left behind can feel dumb for sticking around.

- Don't react to turnover by handing out promotions. Bandaids won't fix the real problem.

- Be careful not to treat certain people better than others just because they complain more.

5.7. Deal with those who should leave

- Engineers need skill and will. Resolving a lack of either is doable, but little can fix a lack of both.

- Engineers enjoy conquering problems. If they drag, they may just be finding the job too difficult.

- Look out for engineers who are complacent. You need to weed out the black boxes in your team.

- Upon recognising a poor performer, meet and tell them, then meet again later to talk objectives.

- If you feel a second chance is being wasted, you might as well start planning the exit interview.

Summary

- Get to know your engineers.
- Hold weekly one-on-ones with them.

- Conduct their annual performance reviews.
- Motivate them.
- Handle their emotional outbursts.
- Deal with those who want to leave.
- Deal with those who should leave.

CHAPTER SIX
The Team

6.1. Develop a culture of excellence in the team

- Create an atmosphere of eliteness, whereby your engineers will think it a step down to leave.

- Encourage an attitude of having fun with "what" they do, while taking pride in "how" they do it.

- Development ≠ Production: A developer's job is to create, think, be unique, and occasionally fail.

- A team rallied behind common goals and principles is far greater than the sum of its parts.

6.2. Get them pulling in the same direction

- Group engineers in 2's or 3's per project, pair top performers with top performers, and so on.

- Separating people of the same functional purpose into cross-functional teams kills shared experience.

- Facilitate decisions, don't dictate them. Help your staff find the answers, then pick the best one.

- Once a decision is made, trust them with it, and monitor non-intrusively. Be careful of plan B's.

- Trust doesn't mean leaving things implicit. Make sure everybody knows what they should be doing.

- Standards should be light, empower developers, and improve productivity, not impede it.

- You build both products and people. Let them do something that's not in the budget now and then.

6.3. Keep communication flowing

- The Tower of Babel had all the resources and time it needed, but poor communication killed it.

- Hold brief status meetings daily. Ask what they did, what they will do, and what they're stuck on.

- Daily status meetings give you the opportunity to let people know what you've been up to as well.

- A good meeting is a debate, has the right people, a definition of "done", a referee, and a notetaker.

- Communication with remote workers is different (video chat, IM, etc.), but should be as constant.

- Find ways to let your staff explain their project to others, either informally, or in presentation form.

- Try to arrange team lunches, and/or meet-ups after-hours to socialise with your team as well.

6.4. Protect them from others

- If the team can see that you're looking out for them, they'll look out for you too.

- Protect your engineers from interruptions by allowing people with queries to come to you first.

- Stand up for your team when people take shots at them, and listen out for any nasty rumours.

- Be a lowpass filter for scheduling noise. Wait for a milestone to inform the team about big changes.

- Your team should feel a part of the company culture, but protect them from any bad influences.

6.5. Protect them from themselves

- Try to avoid internal competition. It makes coaching difficult, and can create harmful tension.

- People can only cover for others who don't put in as much effort (or even overtime) for so long.

- NIH syndrome: Developers would rather stand on the toes of others, than their shoulders.

- The only constant is change. People hate change. The best reaction you can hope for is a debate.

Summary

- Develop a culture of excellence in the team.
- Get them pulling in the same direction.
- Keep communication flowing.
- Protect them from others.
- Protect them from themselves.

PART THREE

Manage Their...

CHAPTER SEVEN
Their Environment

7.1. Recognise an unhealthy work environment

- While a manager's job is interrupt-driven, engineers need stretches of uninterrupted focus.

- If people feel like they're being forced into a mould, they'll do anything to break out of it.

- If your staff feel uncomfortable in their workplace, they'll look for excuses not to be there.

7.2. Create an environment that works

- Your job is not to make people work, but instead

to make it possible for them to do so.

- Combat interruptions actively (remove noise) and passively (provide physical barriers).

- Allow developers to personalise themselves (their clothes) and their workspace (photos, toys, etc.).

- Provide comfort in the form of sufficient space, privacy, and quality furniture and equipment.

- The loss of productivity grossly outweighs the cost of setting up an environment like this.

Summary

- Recognise an unhealthy work environment.
- Create an environment that works.

CHAPTER EIGHT
Their Projects

8.1. Align yourself with the company's strategy

- Before taking on a project, make sure you can understand and get behind the strategy behind it.

- Strategies based on the hindsight analysis of other companies are flawed (Correlation ≠ Cause).

- We live in a messy, unpredictable world. Success is a complex mix of strategy, execution, and luck.

- Execution is at least contained, but even with a flawless strategy, it's still far from predictable.

8.2. Get projects off on the right foot

- A project that is poorly specified, overly complex, poorly estimated, or over-promised is DOA.

- Extract as much information about the client's needs as possible, but define "what", not "how".

- Solutions are 10x more complex than problems. Meet with your engineers to reduce the problem.

- List all features in order of combined risk and importance. Risk is good, but it must be managed.

- Agree on a minimum viable product, and expect that to change, so get it to the client fast.

- Roughly estimate a release schedule. Plan for 1/3 design, 1/6 coding, 1/4 testing, and 1/4 QA.

8.3. Keep development rolling

- Set up and name the project early, it makes it feel more real, and hence, more exciting to work on.

- Tackle features in order of priority, and work with the team to define "done" for each.

- Split each feature into tasks such as: "research", "prototype", "design", "implement", and "test".

- Define "done" for each task, and assign each an estimated complexity rating of: 1, 2, 4, 8, 16.

- Don't be afraid to get your hands dirty. Take on the odd tasks your team doesn't have time for.

- As soon as all essential features are deemed "done", get it into QA, then get it to the client.

8.4. Monitor progress

- You're judged on your ability to deliver quality software within scope, time, and budget.

- Push for quality code, documentation, and tests. I assure you, TDD is a lot cheaper than no testing.

- A task board (digital or physical) can allow you to

assess progress quickly and non-intrusively.

- (combined complexity rating of all "done" tasks) / (time spent on the project) ≈ (work rate).

- To truly measure progress and recognise slippage, you'll need your staff to be honest with you.

- You're a people manager first. In charge but not in control. It goes: people => projects => profits.

- Know when to stop adding new features, and when to declare the project "ready for release".

8.5. Handle disasters

- Projects are rarely high tech, so they rarely fail due to technical reasons. They fail sociologically.

- When disaster strikes, get the team together, and try to completely understand the problem first.

- Time and budget are typically fixed, so when time is running out, reduce scope, not quality.

• Don't blame the team if the project fails, but don't reward them for fighting their own fires either.

Summary

• Align yourself with the company's strategy.
• Get projects off on the right foot.
• Keep development rolling.
• Monitor progress.
• Handle disasters.

ACKNOWLEDGMENTS

A special thank you to all of the inspiring leaders I've had the honour of working with:

Julian Houghton

R&D Manager - IDS

Stilianos Canos

Team Lead - IDS

Richard McKenzie

R&D Manager - ThoroughTec

Rishen Panday

Team Lead - ThoroughTec

Thomas Strehl
R&D Manager - Canonical

Alejandro Cura
R&D Manager - Canonical

Michi Henning
Tech Lead - Canonical

A big thank you also to the great authors who've influenced so much of what went into this book:

Dale Carnegie
How To Win Friends and Influence People

Daniel H. Pink
Drive: The Surprising Truth About What Motivates Us

Edward Yourdon
Death March

Eric Ries
The Lean Startup: How Today's Entrepreneurs Use Continuous Innovation to Create Radically Successful Businesses

Frederick P. Brooks Jr.

The Mythical Man-Month: Essays on Software Engineering

Jonathan Rasmusson

The Agile Samurai: How Agile Masters Deliver Great Software

Joshua Tyler

Building Great Software Engineering Teams: Recruiting, Hiring, and Managing Your Team from Startup to Success

Michael Lopp

Managing Humans: Biting and Humorous Tales of a Software Engineering Manager

Mickey W. Mantle
& Ron Lichty

Managing the Unmanageable: Rules, Tools, and Insights for Managing Software People and Teams

Phil Rosenzweig

The Halo Effect: ... and the Eight Other Business Delusions That Deceive Managers

Rob Goffee
& Gareth Jones
Why Should Anyone Be Led by You?: What It Takes to Be an Authentic Leader

Tom DeMarco
& Tim Lister
Peopleware: Productive Projects and Teams